Ella Fraser Weller

Nestlings

A Collection of Poems

Ella Fraser Weller

Nestlings
A Collection of Poems

ISBN/EAN: 9783744712255

Printed in Europe, USA, Canada, Australia, Japan

Cover: Foto ©Thomas Meinert / pixelio.de

More available books at **www.hansebooks.com**

※

NESTLINGS

※

NESTLINGS

A COLLECTION OF POEMS

BY

ELLA FRASER WELLER

ILLUSTRATED BY

K. A. FRASER

FROM PICTURES OF CHILDREN IN THE AUTHOR'S
IMMEDIATE CIRCLE OF FRIENDS

SAN FRANCISCO
CALIFORNIAN PUBLISHING CO.
1892

LOVINGLY DEDICATED

TO THE CHILDREN WHOSE FACES

ARE

PICTURED WITHIN

INTRODUCTORY

✳

THESE selections have come of occasions. They were not meant for the public eye. The thought of a possible book had given them greater unity, and the vision of a possible critic had probably modified their form. The mother-love for children called for them and they came ; there is a conspiracy of mother-loves and the fugitive poems became a book.

The accompanying illustrations are shadows of real faces and may be readily duplicated in any limited circle.

"Nestlings" may serve as an album for some innocent faces, and perpetuate some possibly helpful sentiment.

S. H. WELLER

Los Angeles, California

List of Illustrations

CONTENTS

✴

"AS I came o'er the distant hills
    I heard a nestling sing :
' Oh, pleasant are the primrose buds
    In the perfumed breath of spring !
And pleasant are the mossy banks
    Beneath the birchen bowers—
But a home wherein no children play
    Is a garden shorn of flowers.' "

"MY BABY'S FEET"

My Baby's Feet

WITHIN my palm, like roseleaves, dainty, sweet,
    I fold with tenderest love two little feet—
Two little feet, twin flow'rets come to bring
To mother's heart the first sweet breath of spring.
Wearied with play, at last they lie at rest,
One satin sole against its fair mate pressed.
Dear little feet, fain would this hand 'ere shield
Thy tender flesh from thorns which lie concealed
Along the path which, stretching through the years,
Leads on to God, through joy and silent tears,
Oh, would that I could pluck from thy dear way
Whate'er might tempt these little feet to stray,
What though my hands be torn by thorn and stone,
Thy joy, for all my pain would soon atone;
If but thy mother planned thy life for thee,
No other path so bright as thine should be.
But what am I, that I my love should count
Greater than that of Him, who is love's fount—
Who sent from heaven, these dainty baby feet
To make thy mother's life and love complete?
What truer hand than His could mark thy path?
What greater love than God, thy Father, hath?
What greater wisdom shields thee from all strife?

What greater mercy grants eternal life?
When shadows come, and clouds obscure thy way
He knows that darkness only heralds day.
If bruised thy flesh, though mother's heart may bleed,
He, in His mercy, knows thy greatest need.
Then, little feet, though mother's prayers may rise,
In love and trust, that never doubt implies
That God, thy steps may lead in ways aright,
And keep thy soul from sin's unholy blight,
I'll leave thy future in His hands alone,
And know, at last, He'll bring thee safely home.

Two Little Seeds

TWO little seeds sank deep in the earth,
    Down through the narrow darkening way,
Side by side in a slow descent,
    Away from the light, on an April day.
Two little seeds—you scarce could tell
    One from the other—both brown and round,
Planted, that day by the self-same hand
    In the mellow depths of the self-same ground.
Nestling together they chattered thus,
    As close in their cozy nest they lay :
"What are we here for down in the dark
    Hidden so deep from the light of day ? "
"What are we here for ? I, for one,"
    Said the first little seed, in a gruesome tone,
" Shall just go to sleep, and sleep right on,
    Close by the side of this round smooth stone.
I shall not stir, but I'll sweetly sleep,
    Until old Mother Earth must surely see
That here, in the damp of the chilly ground,
    Is never the place for the like of me."
Proud and idle, it went to sleep,
    And it slept right on, though the warm rain fell,

And Nature found, when she came to look,
  Nothing at all but an empty shell.
The other seed mused-—"It cannot be right
  Thus in the earth to so idly lie,
This life of ours will wasted be
  And soon in this gloom, unused, must die.
I shall not sleep—from this narrow shell
  I'll find my way, and out of this night
I shall reach right up, until day by day
  I nearer and nearer approach the light.
Already I feel the welcome heat
  Warming the loam that around me lies,
Already I see in my sweetest dreams
  The genial sun and the azure skies.
Oh! slumber then in your slothful ease,
  By your foolish fancies alone deceived,
While the grandest victories Earth e'er knew
  Are only waiting to be achieved."
So out from his shell the wee seed burst,
  And stretched to the full of its graceful length,
While the light and warmth of the Summer sun
  Added each day to its beauty and strength.
Its slender fingers of tender green
  Catches the trellis here and there,
Higher and higher reaching up,
  Branching out in the Summer air.

Oh, fair are the blossoms it bears for all,
 And fragrant the breath of its golden bells ;
Glad is the music they ring for you,
 From the perfumed depths where the dewdrop dwells.
They wake you out of your sluggish sleep—
 Their voices are ringing—Arise ! Arise !
God gave you your life to use for Him,
 And can you the gift of a King despise ?
Your strength will waste if it is not used,
 The life He has lent He will ask again,
Can you bring but the empty shell to Him,
 And tell Him His gift has been in vain ?

" EDITH "

Edith

ONE flower within my garden grows—
　　My friend's is crowded,
But mine is rarer than the rose,
　　My skies unclouded.
I shield it when the north winds blow
　　So harsh across it,
I cannot let them kiss it so,
　　And rudely toss it.

So beautiful it is and frail,
　　I almost dread
The butterflies that soar and sail
　　So near its bed.
I envy not the wealth of flowers
　　Across the way ;
My radiant flower exhales perfume
　　For me each day.

My gratitude to Heaven for this,
　　My one late flower ;
And such a sense of rapturous bliss
　　Ascends each hour.

Dear Heaven, still a gift bestow
   And grant to me
The grace to train my flower to grow
   For Heaven and Thee.

And yet, because I love it so
   My heart will fail,
When life's rude tempests 'gin to blow
   My blossom frail.
Help me to shield it from the rain—
   From winter's blast—
And I will give it back again
   To Thee at last.

The Theft

A CROW flew down from a tall oak tree,
    Just as important as he could be;
For a Congress of birds was to meet that day,
And he had determined to have his say.
He plumed his feathers and looked severe,
As the birds flew in from far and near.
A Mocking Bird sat on a limb near by,
With a desperate look in his round, dark eye;
He was the culprit —a thief he had been,
The Thrush and the Blackbird had "run him in."
He had stolen the nest of the little brown Wren
From the tangled depth of a shady glen.
The Hawk was the Judge, and sat in state,
Ready to seal the prisoner's fate.
"A thief is worse," said the Bobolink,
"Than anything else on earth, I think."
But—"Order in Court"—rang close to his ear,
Robin, the Sheriff, was standing near.
Then the Crow began in his deep sub-bass,
And his pompous manner to plead the case.
He spoke of the prisoner's youth at first,
But a murmur of scorn from the audience burst,
So he changed his tactics and said: "I hear

Of late the prisoner has acted queer.
In fact, I can make it to you quite plain
That most of his ancestors were insane.
Young as he is, and with such a taint,
'Tis folly to make against him complaint."
He talked till the Mocking Bird felt secure,
Feeling acquittal was coming sure.
Then the Owl rose up, and his blinking eyes,
Droll and uncanny, looked wondrous wise :
"Tu whit, tu whoo ! You will find it vain
To plead that the prisoner 's now insane;
Insane, did you say ? Oh, well, perhaps—
But there is a prison for all such chaps,
The Mocking Bird's record has always been
Soiled and blotted by many a sin.
If this were the first of his insane tricks—
But the family trait to the fellow sticks.
Only last week—but you all have heard—
How he broke up the home of the Humming Bird.
Stealing and hiding the theft by a lie
Is the poorest rule for a bird to try.
We have borne with him for many a year,
But now we must act. Have I made it clear ?"
And he loudly read from the law a clause,
Then flew to his perch, amid loud applause.
The charge to the jury was something fine,

Pathos and power in every line.
They were out but a moment, then entered again,
Nor had the eloquent charge been vain ;
For the verdict "Guilty," rang out clear,
Filling the pris'ner with abject fear.
Then the Judge rose up, and shaking his head,
Solemnly, thus the sentence read :
" Let every bird from yon prisoner's breast,
A feather pluck for the Wren's new nest."
Scarce had they heard the words pronounced
Ere they all in a mob on the culprit pounced,
Each plucking a feather, he flew to the glen
Eager to comfort the poor little Wren.
The Mocking Bird shivered with cold and pain,
"Oh ! never," he cried, "will I steal again,
And I'll try, oh! I'll try to do what is right,
Nor ever be found in such a sad plight."
The dear, gentle Dove, who had lingered behind,
Came close to the prisoner, loving and kind,
And she whispered so low, "Come home to my nest ;
I'll care for you tenderly, give you my best.
I know you are sorry, I know you will try,
So come, let us home to my warm nest fly."
So nursed by the Dove, one fair summer day,
He kissed her and blessed her, and then flew away.
But whether he truly became a good bird

I'm sure I can't say, as I never have heard.
But I know on his record there'll ever remain,
Though the act be repented, its dark, ugly stain;
And he'll find o'er and o'er such tricks do not pay,
For punishment comes, and oft comes to stay.
No matter how small is the act that we do,
This thing, little children, you'll find always true:
That somehow or some way it does come about,
The wrong that we do will soon find us out,
And we're filled with such sorrow and in such a plight,
We see very clearly, "'Tis best to do right."

"WHO'S AFRAID"

Who's Afraid

RUN, little man, or old Jack Frost
  Will catch you ere you know it,
I am sure you are half afraid of him,
  Though your manner does not show it.

With your soft warm cap and your overcoat,
  You think you can safely meet him.
The harsh old fellow will have to look sharp,
  Or the coy little man will cheat him.

See how bravely he faces the piercing wind,
  Not afraid of the cold is he,
And the roses bloom on his rounded cheek,
  As he romps in his boyish glee.

Heigh-ho, little man, if you meet the storms,
  That blow o'er the hills of life,
With half the courage you show to-day,
  You are sure to win in the strife.

Then go, little man, and never you fear
  But look the world in the face,
And you'll find on the heights of life, my boy,
  That world will make you a place.

'Tis only the brave that fortune finds,
  'Tis only the good who win;
The sluggards' bulwarks are tumbled down,
  And he falls in the gutters of sin.

So up, little man, and never say fail,
  Though frosts of adversity fall;
With courage your armor, and hope for a sword,
  There is naught your heart can appall.

Lullaby

SLUMBER sweet, noddlekins,
   Nurse is full of prickly pins,
Mamma's full of kisses sweet
For dimpled hands and rosy feet.

Slumber comes—close your eyes,
Angels watch you from the skies,
Little dreams come drifting down
To veil those roguish eyes of brown.

Nestling close on Mamma's arm,
You are safe from every harm.
Close I clasp you—all my joy,
Centers in you—darling boy.

Now your eyelid fringes meet,
Kissed by slumbers, soft and sweet.
Who can wonder, angels keep
Tender watch when babies sleep ?

For I'm sure no lovelier sight
Ever graces realms of light,
They are golden links of love
Binding earth to Heaven above.

Sleep, my baby, sleep and rest,
Nestled close on Mother's breast ;
Harm can never reach you here,
God and Mother guard you, dear.

Two of Them

WHERE is the little boy Tommy ?
Not in the parlor with hammer and tacks,
Not in the kitchen with sharp little axe,
Not on the lawn where patient old Bose
Lies half asleep with a fly on his nose ;
Not in the garden planting his seeds,
Pulling up flowers as often as weeds,
        No little Tommy.

Nor in the barn do I see his short legs,
Climbing the ladder to hunt for the eggs ;
Nor yet in the meadow where cowslips are yellow,
Half hid by the grass, do I see the wee fellow,
I am sure he was here but a moment ago—
I wonder why boys are gotten up so !
        Queer little Tommy.

Oh ! down in the orchard where apples are green
A moment ago Master Tommy was seen—
High in the top of a gnarled old tree
Stuffing his pockets, and hiding from me ;
Playing me tricks, for he knows full well
That his mamma's away, and that I won't tell.
I won't tell, and you wonder why ?
Well, Tommy's a boy—and so was I.

" IN THE MEADOW "

In the Meadow.

I HEARD the grasses talking, talking,
　Down in the meadow, one summer day,
The prettiest things I heard them whisper,
　Nodding their heads in a quaint wise way.

Whether they knew that I was listening,
　And would tell to you their story sweet,
I know not ; but surely they would not chide me ;
　For the gossiping winds their words repeat.

They told how they loved the golden sunshine ;
　How once in the gloom of a strange long night
They feared they were lost, until angel fingers
　Touched them with life, and they found the light.

And how the tints of emerald landscape
　Were caught from the sunlight on cloud and sky;
How dewdrops, gems from the crystal fountains,
　Were showered o'er earth from realms on high.

I heard them say, how the cowslips yellow
　Were bits of the sun, dropped here and there -
How the lilies pure, with their snow white petals,
　Were down from the wings of angels fair.

And the blue-eyed violets, shy and tender,
  With breath from the censer of heaven sent,
Were bits of the sky, by the summer borrowed,
  And just for the season to Flora lent.

They told how the daisies and buttercups yellow,
  Marked where the feet of the swift hours trod;
When fickle they fled from the pussy-willow,
  To the newer love of the golden rod.

How the bolder touches of gorgeous color
  From the crimson glory of sunset came,
And touching with blood the swaying poppies,
  Set hill and valley and field aflame.

Oh, they told me things that set me thinking,
  Thoughts that never were mine before ;
And the love of Christ for his wayward children
  Filled me with wonder more and more.

How even the flowers and grasses know Him,
  How He loves and cares for their needs alway,
That they take no thought for the coming morrow,
  But live and trust in the bright to-day.

And may not we, who are Christ's own Children,
  Blotting the present with anxious tears,
Live our joy, and leave to His mercy
  The shadowy doubts of future years ?

The somber gloom of the distant mountain
   Reveals no path that our feet may tread,
But at its foot upwinding ever
   It stretches out like a silver thread.

Down in the meadows, among the grasses,
   My pillow of daisies and violets blue,
The sweetest stories of all the summer
   I hear, and come and whisper to you.

I may not tell you all they told me.
   Go press your ear to the fragrant sod—
The pulse that beats in Nature's bosom
   Throbs in the heart of Nature's God.

Beatrice

DIMPLED hands and dimpled cheeks,
    Dimpled chin beguiling ;
Rows of gleaming, pearly teeth,
    Rosy lips a smiling.

Rings of dark and shining hair,
    Around a white brow clinging ;
Hazel eyes where gladness shines,
    And sets the heart to singing.

Dainty feet with dimpled toes,
    Little hands caressing ;
Gurgling laugh and lisping tongue
    Helplessness confessing.

Roguish glances, sidelong, sweet,
    What is Baby doing?
Face half hidden in my breast,
    All my kisses wooing.

Softly, softly slumber comes,
    See her eyes are closing ;
Cupid, shorn of bow and wings,
    In my arms reposing.

Blessed home where baby comes,
 What a void without her ;
Joy and love and sunshine bright,
 Lingers all about her.

Not a shadow comes to me,
 But at once 'tis lifted,
Just because this Baby sweet,
 Down from Heaven drifted.

" MY BOY "

My Boy

OH, where did you come from, baby mine,
　　With your face like a cherub's sweet?
Did the angels scatter with flowers, the path
　That was pressed by your little feet?
Or, did you fly from the realms of love?
　On your shoulders methinks I see
In the crumpled roseleaf dimples there,
　The place where the wings should be.
The angels were loth to leave you, my child,
　I know they were filled with fear,
I almost fancy I hear their wings
　Hovering somewhere near.
Oh, they need not doubt that your mother's heart
　Holds less of love than their own,
And though I may lack of their wisdom my pet,
　My love for the lack shall atone.
Oh, gift of the angels—Gift of God,
　What a trust for a mortal to hold!
A boy to guide in the paths of right,
　A soul for Heaven to mold.
My darling, I fain would shelter you here,
　Close, close on my own fond breast,

For my heart shrinks back from the terrors of life
  When my bird flies out of the nest.
If only Christ gave me the power, my boy,
  To suffer and toil in your stead,
I'd pluck every thorn from your path in life
  And toss you its roses instead.
And the selfish love of your mother, boy,
  Would rob you of life's best boon,
And drown the chorus of angel choirs,
  By setting the world attune.
So I'll send back the tears of a mother's love,
  I will crush out a mother's fear,
And push you with tender, trembling hands
  Out into Life's highway, dear.
Yet strongly armored by truth, my boy,
  And shod by your mother's prayer,
I'll know that your Heavenly Father's love
  O'ershadows you everywhere.
And that sometime, after life's battle is o'er
  In the land of our promised rest—
I shall meet you, my baby, to part never more,
  And hold you once more on my breast.

The Fairy's Motto

A FAMILY of Fairies lived under the ground,
And search as they might no place co'd be found,
Where a home they could make, a snug little nest,
A refuge from harm when by foes they were pressed.
Day in, and day out they skurried about,
Putting fish worms, and beetles, and such like to rout.
At length one, the most energetic of all,
Found something quite large and round like a ball,
So calling the family, with pickaxe and spades
They soon in the wonder an opening made.
And what do you think they found it to be?
A turnip so large it might have been three.
So they hollowed it out as fast as they could,
Not pausing a moment for rest or for food.
A part of the contents they hurled from the door,
And trampled the rest to thicken the floor,
And ere through the holes the sun 'gan to peep,
The turnip was empty, the Fairies asleep.
The gardener on passing his turnip bed saw,
'Midst the flourishing green a queer looking flaw:
"Why, how can this be? I'm sure yester-e'en,
That turnip, as any, was thrifty and green.
There may be a grub at its root, or perhaps,

A bug at its top, they are meddlesome chaps;
I'll wait until morning, the heat of the sun
May have proven too much for a delicate one."
In the meantime the Fairies waked up by his words,
Laughed and chuckled together as happy as birds.
"Before he comes round, we'll have finished and done,
And he'll find that his turnip is not worth a bun.
He will leave it and we will hold revelry high,
For that some may have life, why, something must die."
So they cut a small hole through the top, for a door,
The tiniest roots from the outside they tore,
And made them a ladder, so firm and so fair
It answered their purpose and served as a stair.
A cabbage leaf carpet, a bedstead so neat
They made in a minute, just out of a beet,
A table and chairs were made out of roots,
Supported in style by asparagus shoots.
Lace curtains of spider webs, hung o'er the doors,
And bumble bee skins were the rugs on the floors,
Their dishes were all from the button weed made,
Their knives and their forks from the tiny grass blade,
Corn silk for their cushions, thistledown for a bed,
"Our home will be royal," they boastingly said.
They caught a black cricket and hollowed him out,
For a crib the sweet baby must have, without doubt,
And the cricket, his life, ought gladly to give,
For "something must die, that others may live."

But why should I tell you the wonderful way
They furnished and finished their house the next day ?
They sent invitations to their four hundred friends—
" At Home—after sunset until the night ends."
But plans that are made for ends of our own,
May steal our sweet plums and leave us the stone.
Next day as the gardener walked down through the rows
Pressing down the soft earth here and there with his toes,
He found that the turnip looked worse than before —
And grimly he smiled, for he saw the top door,
That the Fairies forgot in their hurry last night
To close with the curtains, and fasten down tight,
So stooping, he gathered the leaves dry and dead,
Gave a vigorous pull, and away o'er his head
He sent it a-flying—Poor Fairies, good-bye—
" That something may live, you know, something must
    die."

" A REVERIE "

A Reverie

STANDING to-night beside their little bed,
   All richly hung with tapestry and lace,
I look half sadly down upon my treasures there,
My boys, so full of innocence and grace,
My little lambs, safe folded for the night,
Caught by the god of slumber unaware.
The sturdy lad's soft cheek close pressed
Against his baby brother's, soft and fair ;
The smile is still upon the boy's red mouth,
On baby's face the roguish dimples lie ;
The curls of brown, the shining rings of gold,
Like sun and shadow tremble as I sigh—
Sigh that so much of innocence and grace
So soon must leave a mother's tender care—
So soon the hurrying years crowd on apace,
And bring to each of toil and pain his share.
To-day, when poisoned breath from lips profane,
Blown harshly from the busy street below,
Entered my safe retreat, and brought
Quick to my side the lad, his cheeks aglow,
His hazel eyes with wonder wide met mine ;
I could not speak—I stooped and kissed his hand.
The shadow passed, my heart leaped up in joy—

The words—the sin—he did not understand,
But ere the cloud had left his childish face
Upon my heart this deeper shadow lay :
I cannot always keep my darlings safe :
They'll leave the shelter of the fold some day.
Strong-willed, strong-hearted, loving boys—
Harmonious souls by angels set attune—
Oh, may my fingers touch the keys aright !
I ask of Heaven than this no greater boon ;
No greater boon than wisdom from on high
To strengthen them against the snares of sin ;
To teach them how to live and how to die,
To hear their Master bid them " Enter in ! "
So, with my good-night kiss upon your lips
I'll banish all the shadows from my heart,
And know He'll send His blessed sunshine in,
If only you and I will do *our* part.

My Choice

I'M only a boy, but before me lie
   Life's paths untrod, and a sunny sky
Bends o'er the paths, and smiles on me.
And under its blue serene, I see
Two ways stretch out, one, narrow and straight ;
The other, broad, and an open gate
Beckons me on, and smiling and sweet
Are the Heavens fair, and down at my feet
Fair flowers bloom, and the grasses nod
On the level slope of the emerald sod.
In the bosky dells my eyes discern
The feathery flakes of the filmy fern,
The birds' low song in the shadows deep
Lull my fancies to dreamful sleep.
The sun-flecked slopes and the open gate
Seem for my eager feet to wait.
But the narrow way, though rough and steep,
Has a charm for me, and my senses leap
As I view the heights that seem to rise
From the lowly earth, to the sunlit skies.
Though rough and steep, and with danger fraught,
Though the glorious heights with my life be bought—
I'll turn from the broad road leading down,

And seek the heights and the laurel crown.
From the blood-stained prints of my thorn-pierced feet,
Spring wonderful flowers, whose fragrance sweet,
Borne on the breath of the balmy air,
Charms my heart and dispels my care.
The beetling crags that block my way,
The storm cloud's gloom, where the lightnings play,
But give me strength for each new emprise,
And joys my soul as I slowly rise ;
For snares and cliffs, to a boy like me
Should only incentives to action be.
I'm bound to rise—If I earnestly try
I know I can reach the hilltops high.
But I have no time to loiter and play,
On the tempting slopes of the downward way,
But must follow the path, by good men trod,
To rise to the heights of life and God.

Elliott

DEAR little cherub, from isles of the blest,
  What is your destiny? What is your quest?
Have you been watching us with your bright eyes
Till you thought you would come as a cunning surprise?
Did you see that this house lacked a baby so sweet
To widen the circle and make it complete?
Did you see from your perch in the realms up above
The sweet mother-heart overflowing with love?
You thought it so precious, you flew to her breast,
You sought it and found it, and found, too, your rest—
Your refuge from sorrow ; your fortress so strong,
May you rest in it, dwell in it, cherish it long.
You are welcome as dewdrops when parched are the
    flowers ;
You will brighten the days till they shrink into hours.
May heaven watch over you, fill you with joy,
And bless the whole circle, in you, little boy.

"THREE LITTLE KITTENS"

Three Little Kittens

THREE little kittens, black, white and gray,
　　Went out in the garden one morning to play.
Said the white one, " I want to play hide and go seek
'Tis long since we played it, much more than a week."
" All right," said the gray, " I'm ready for fun,"
And he started away with a hop and a run.
" Just wait," said the black with an ominous growl,
His face wrinkled up in the crookedest scowl.
" It's an old-fashioned game—I shan't play at that,
It is not becoming a stylish young cat ;
I'll sport with the leaves or I'll play in the sun,
But it's tiresome, unpleasant and foolish to run."
The others agreed in a good-natured way,
And the three little kittens began then to play ;
The dead leaves went flying to right and to left,
All three, for a time seemed of senses bereft ;
But something went wrong—" I say that's not fair,"
The black kitten cried—" and to play I don't care"—
The gray and the white coaxed him hard for awhile,
But nothing would cause him to speak or to smile,
So they left him alone and hied them away—
" Hide and seek " mongst the roses and lilacs to play.
He heard their gay laughter and sullener grew—

The sun was too hot—the skies were too blue,
The grass, he was certain, was damp where he lay,
All things had conspired to annoy him that day,
He could bear neither sunshine, the mirth that he heard,
The hum of the bees, nor the chirp of a bird.
How silly they seemed—it made him so cross—
The pleasures of life were nothing but dross,
So he hastened away in a fit of despair ;
All things were against him and " nothing was fair."
And now, little people, does any one know
A child who is cross, and always acts so ?
Who cries with a pout—" I say I shan't play,
Unless you do everything just as I say."
If beaten at games, he says " It's not fair"—
And takes of good things far more than his share.
If you know such a child, I'm sure you will find
He is sour and unhappy, because he's unkind ;
To be happy, be gentle, good tempered and sweet
To playmates and elders and all whom you meet.

What is the Use of Trying?

"WHAT is the use of trying?
    I never can learn to fly,
See how the lark goes floating
    Up to the sunlit sky ;
He never failed as I have,
    See how he flies at ease,
Light as a down of thistle
    Tossed on the tremulous breeze.
I have been foolishly trying,
    Thinking I, too, might rise,
I'll stay down here in the hedges,
    And leave to the lark the skies."
So he stayed in the crowded hedges,
    And lived through the summer long,
Only a common sparrow—
    One of a common throng.
" What is the use of trying?
    Pouring o'er book and slate,
I fail, and shall keep on failing,
    For men are created great.
'Tis folly to think that study

For so many hours a day
Is going to make out of boys and girls,
   Wise women and men alway.
So what is the use of trying ?
   A common lot shall be mine ;
Why muddle my brain with study ?
   I never was meant to shine ; "
So away in the closet cupboard
   The books kept gathering dust,
And the mind they were meant to nourish
   Was buried and lost in rust.
So the hedges go gathering sparrows,
   And the larks still mount to the sky,
And out from the crowded byways
   Few souls gain the mountains high.
Have courage and keep on trying,
   Though a sparrow, a lark cannot be,
The highways that lead to the Pisgahs
   Are open to you and to me.

"ONLY FIVE"

Only Five

I' VE had a birthday party—
   Of course I'm only five—
But I had the jolliest time
   Of any boy alive.
I got some little chickens,
   The roosters cannot crow ;
But on my mamma's table
   I stand them in a row.

I got the funniest bank—
   A man, all mouth and eyes,
He swallows every penny,
   And every dime he spies ;
My mamma set a dinner
   For Ollie and for me.
'Twas just a *little* party,
   One little girl, you see.

We had the nicest oranges,
   And nuts, and apples red,
And just the tiniest custard pie,
   Plum cake and snow white bread.

We ate up all we wanted,
  Mamma sat by and smiled,
And kissed my curls and dimples,
  And called me " precious child."

And when the day was over,
  And I was snug in bed,
She found the *prettiest* book I have,
  And lots of stories read :
And then—I can't remember,
  My head was in a mix :
For when the sand-man found me,
  I dreamed that I was six.

Unreconciled

HID away in the corner I found it,
   A little shoe worn out and old ;
But dearer to me in my sorrow
   Than all earth's treasures of gold.
Scarcely lost to the foot's soft imprint,
   I can fancy its warmth still there
As I press it close, close to my bosom
   And sob in my hopeless despair.
My arms are so useless and empty,
   My heart is so hungry and sore,
My dear little golden-haired baby,
   Will lie on my breast, nevermore.
Nevermore, will I feel the soft pressure
   Of his rosy lips pressed against mine,
Nevermore will his arms warm and tender
   My neck with caresses entwine.
You mock when you say God has ta'en him
   Away from the sorrows of earth,
What love could shelter and shield him,
   Like the love that had given him birth ?
Will it heal the mad longing to fold him

Once more to my grief-stricken heart,
To tell me I'll meet him in Heaven
  Nevermore from my darling to part?
Your words are well meant, I can feel it,
  But the wound is too deep and too fresh,
I cannot deal now with the spirit,
  Oh! God give him back in the flesh.
Let me see him again as I saw him,
  So winsome, so rosy, so bright,
His baby face dimpled and roguish,
  His blue eyes with laughter alight,
Let me feel in my mad desolation,
  His heart throbbing close to my own,
Does God pity me in my sorrow?
  Does he care for my heartbroken moan?
Had he need of my darling in Heaven
  That the life of my life he has ta'en?
Do not try, while my poor heart is breaking
  The mystery of death to explain,
Let me sit by myself in the shadow,
  Let me kiss as I will the worn shoe;
For I'm chilled by the breath of the angel
  That over my hearthstone flew.
Let me weep as I will, and the teardrops
  May wash from my dim eyes away

The shadows that hide in their garments,
 · The light and the glory of day.
Perhaps, as you say, Christ is tender,
  And he'll shelter my lamb in his breast,
But your sympathy hurts me, I cannot—
  I will not say yet—" It is best."

" THE NAUGHTY DOLLY "

The Naughty Dolly

"OH, Dolly! How can you be naughty?
        You've been naughty the whole day through;
You spoiled your white dress in the gutter,
    And stuck up my pictures with glue;
And when in a corner I put you,
    And plead with you so to be good,
You stared in my face with a simper,
    And acted so saucy and rude.
I have tried so hard to be patient—
    For I'm sorry to punish you so;
And I love you, my poor naughty Dolly,
    Much more than you ever can know.
I hope you will think the day over;
    I am going to bed now—good-night.
Be a good little Dolly to-morrow,
    And try all the day to do right."

Mabel's Lesson

MABEL, stood by the garden gate
   Swinging her hat in a careless way ;
A frown on her face, a pout on her lip ;
   For naughty had Mabel been that day.

A pert brown Thrush on a bough o'er head
   Fluttered his wings and carolled his song.
Happy as ever a bird could be,
   Singing and working all day long.

Mabel had risen late that morn ;
   The breakfast was over, and everything cold ;
Mamma was busy and Harry was ill,
   And Bridget did nothing at all but scold.

Long ere the light, the Thrush had been out,
   Catching his breakfast as best he could ;
Working and singing with right good will—
   Never was bird in a merrier mood.

Mabel had started the day all wrong,
   Had hurriedly dressed and forgotten to pray ;
The bird sang on and she heard his song,
   And the wonderful things he seemed to say.

" I waked," he sang, " as one by one
   The stars slipped out of the purple night,
Ere the slender fingers of infant dawn
   Could catch the thread of their faint pure light.

I bathed in the brook that sings near by,
   And borne on the breath of the opening day,
Joyously up to the brightening sky,
   I sent to my Maker a grateful lay.

And so I go on and I build my nest,
   Happy and busy as bird can be ;
For I know though the winds blow cold and chill,
   My Heavenly Father guardeth me."

Mabel looked up with a penitent face,
   The bird had flown, but the lesson stayed,
And Mabel went in from the garden gate
   A better, and wiser, and happier maid.

For bright, or dark is this life of ours,
   Just as we make it, children dear —
With naughty deeds come the chilling showers
   While the skies of the good are bright and clear.

Baby Kathleen

INTO my life, out of Paradise,
   She came like a bird, and the low-hung skies
With the muttered threats of their tempest cloud,
That had covered my life with its dismal shroud
Vanished like dew, when the new day springs
From her rosy couch, and unfolds her wings.
Unfolds her wings for her airy flight
From the mist hung dawn to the purple night,
She hovered so near I could almost reach—
My trembling heart was o'erfull for speech,
When joy! oh! joy, on my throbbing breast
She folded her wings for a moment to rest,
For a moment the gates of pearl were ajar
All earth was alight with the radiant star,
That shone o'er Bethlehem's manger low,
On that wonderful night of the long ago.
But I recked for naught of the glowing skies,
While the lovelight shone from her starry eyes ;
But my beautiful song bird, blithe and free
With her plumage white was too fair for me,
Adown through the shining gates there came

Voices of angels, calling her name.
I had felt the thrill that her presence brought,
I had learned the lesson her love had taught,
She came, and my life was a garden fair,
She fled, and that life was a desert bare,
But my beautiful bird I will find once more
When I wing my flight to the far off shore,
And Heaven, Ah ! Heaven will be so bright
When I find my bird with her plumage white,
When I look once more in her starry eyes,
I shall know I have entered Paradise.

." TWO BOYS "

Two Boys

TWO boys beside my knee
    With eyes so dark and deep;
Two snow-white souls, the God of Love
    Has given to me to keep.
My cup of joy o'er-ran
    That Summer's day,
I knew they were my own—
    My own alway.
My fair twin boys—Ah ! me,
    I look for you
Out o'er life's trodden paths,
    And turn anew
To Him, who never yet
    Has failed to hear
A mother's prayer for those
    She holds so dear.
Oh ! eyes so dark and sweet,
    May Heaven's light
Shine o'er the paths you tread
    And make them bright.
You could not go astray—

For all along
A wall of prayer, I build
  So high and strong,
The tempters cannot scale
  Its dizzy height,
And lead my darlings out,
  To endless night.
These dimpled baby hands
  God gave to you
Through rock-ribbed hills of life
  Their way to hew.
Nor would I, though I might
  Save you the test ;
For well I know, beyond
  Lies Heaven and rest.
This kiss, a pledge I give
  To live for you ;
And know full well, that God
  The rest will do.